Causes of Modern Islamic Terrorism in the West:

Deliberate Deception and Disdain

Dr. Kenneth R. Adderley

DEDICATION

Dedicated to my grandchildren
and thirty-one students in Dr. A's History class

CONTENTS

ACKNOWLEDGMENTS

I acknowledge the encouragement given to me by my brothers Richard and Philip, who encouraged me silently, even while wondering, no doubt, if pen would ever get to paper, and the book written.

Introduction

On September 11, 2001, I was teaching an eight o'clock history class to a group of University Freshmen on a new chapter, which just happened to be entitled the Rise of Islam. The class, although scheduled to finish at 9:15, never happened because sometime around 9 o'clock someone burst through the doors and shouted, "a plane just crashed into the World Trade Center and everyone is rushing into the TV room."

Thirty-one students and I crowded into the viewing space in time to see a second plane and a second crash. I remember saying out loud, "this is no accident . . . and it will be messy." The look of two white history teachers threw a handful of daggers into the eyes of this black professor. Apparently, they too, had immediately surmised that the plane crashes had to be an act of terrorism – something POTUS (President of the United States) Donald J. Trump vehemently insists on referring to fifteen years later as 'Radical Islamic Terrorism,' which he does in order to manipulate voter sympathy for his cause.

Later that morning, several students asked my opinion of what we had spent almost two hours watching gathered around the television set in room

2B. I hesitated, but said that although it was definitely an act of terrorism, I could think of no reason why a Mexican drug cartel would go to such lengths. Thus, based on my knowledge and experience, a logical conclusion had to be that it was an act of war against the United States by some country with a grievance. We now know that 19 Saudis under the banner of Osama bin Laden's al Qaeda, operating out of Afghanistan, had struck at the heart of America's global economy. We would not know that for several weeks.

Many weeks later when we were told that it was an Islamic act of war, my students asked why would they do this, and why do they "hate us so much" that this murder of innocent people is all they could think of doing. After all, we feed most of the world, and we give huge amounts of money to the United Nations and the other economic operations. "Why, why, why?" they asked. "Why do they hate us that much?" That question has plagued me every week since then.

In order to answer that question, the reader must take a history refresher course and try to understand the truth of some bad political decisions made by the Americans and the British during the years of World War I. Many Americans have been duped by the rhetoric of politicians seeking the sweet life of congressional luxury in Washington, who continue to

muddy the waters of the truth, and would even re-write the history of the Middle East if they could do so to be re-elected. It is therefore the thrust of this monograph to shed some light on this darkened conflict by recounting a few of the reasons for the Islamic fight against the West that I have found in the pages of history. A few of these reasons could be listed as: the McMahon Letters (1915); the Sykes-Picot Secret Agreement between
Britain and France (1916); the Balfour Declaration (1917); and the
Mandate System of the League of Nations (1922)

Although it is common knowledge today that the world is at an impasse for several decades trying to forge a solution to the Palestinian-Israeli conflict, many Americans are ignorant at best of some legitimate reasons the Palestinians and Muslims in general may have to be antagonistic toward the West and America in particular.

In addition, the misinformation and western parsing of the signed legal documents coupled with the hidden agenda of political rhetoric from American politicians and British jingoists continue to muddy the waters and present an askant public view. For example, if during the years of occupation in Algiers and Morocco the French military brutalized and killed Arabs at will, would not the grandchildren and great grandchildren of murdered parents who themselves feel denied of justice and opportunity turn out to be killers in France decades later? Apparently, this is exactly what happened in France a few years ago following the Right-wing crackdown against the black children of French Somalia, Morocco, Algiers, and Sierra Leone, and the banning of women's head-scarf.

Now, as of this writing, the new French President, Emmanuel Macron, having defeated the hard-liners on the Right, must come to grips with a situation brought on by decades of French misconduct in the Muslim world. But he also has an opportunity to overcome the winds of terror in France by openly acknowledging the insults of the past, and moving to bridge the ever-increasing suffering of the children they created by French occupation and colonization of the past years in Algiers and Morocco, just like they did in Indochina.

Another question might be, "how much do my students know about the Wahhabi doctrine of Saudi Arabia? And how can they know if their teacher does not know much himself?" Suffice it to say that the adage "what you don't know can hurt you" is quite a true saying in many instances. What I do know of Wahhabism as a history professor, however, is only what I have read from the textbook published by the McGraw-Hill Global Studies series *Islam and the Muslim World* edited by Mir Zohar Husain,

Associate Professor in the Department of Political Science and Criminal Justice at the University of South Alabama. "In 2003, Longman Publishers published the second edition of his book, Global Islamic Politics, and he has presented many papers at professional conferences and lectured on a broad spectrum of global events and issues. . ." (p, v)

Wahhabism is a very strict and puritanical form of Sunni Islam. The easiest way I can explain this idea to students is that just as Christianity had its civil wars and conflicts of purifying its doctrines throughout the centuries, and just as Judaism also had its civil conflicts among themselves as they searched for one authentic Talmudic code, so Islam is now engaged in a long doctrinal conflict ever since Ali died and the Muslim community continues to search for a leader. The dispute over who would be the supreme leader of Islam, however, skewed the practice of a pure faith. The followers of Ali ibn Abi Talib (the Prophet's first cousin and son-in-law) are called Shi'a, while those opting for a **ulama** or **umma** solution and follow the sayings of Prophet Muhammed ibn Abdullah are called Sunni. The Sunnis claim that when the Prophet died he did not designate a successor to lead the **umma** (community of believers); but the Shi'a claim that after Muhammed completed his last **hajj**, he stopped at a place between Makkah and Madina and designated

Ali to be the first Imam on "divine command because Ali was the most righteous." (p, 17)

The Wahhabi code of law and conduct is modeled on that of the original Islamic community established at Makkah and Madina by the Prophet Muhammed. But although the code has been relaxed in modern times it remains the strict code and doctrine of Saudi Arabia today. As a result, Saudi Arabia, where Donald Trump flies this month, is more conservative and puritanical than many other Islamic societies including those in the Persian Gulf (Iraq, Iran). What Americans do not know is that "the Taliban, the Islamic fundamentalist movement that held power in Afghanistan from 1996 to 2001, is thus far the only [ones] in Islam to have embraced Wahhabism." (Husain, 229) But how did Wahhabism originate? What is the origin of this strict form of Islam? Perhaps President Trump would get better answers for his fight against "Radical Islamic Terrorism" than former President George Bush got when he last walked the gardens with King Abdullah ibn Abu Aziz ibn Abdul Rahman al-Saud in 2003/4

Let us examine the origin of the Saudi Nation, which goes back to the eighteenth century. The tribe of Saud roamed the desert beyond the control of the Ottoman Empire. Its leader, Muhammad ibn Saud, wanted to gain an advantage over his rivals in the constant search for water and good grazing lands for the animals. He approached a religious scholar named Abd al-Wahhab, who lived in an oasis near Riyadh, the present Saudi capital. Abd al-Wahhab promised Allah's blessing in return for protection from threats made by the opponents of the strict doctrines he taught, who had threatened to kill him. Thus, they formed a partnership which gave rise to a crusading religious movement called Wahhabism. According to this doctrine, the government of Saudi Arabia maintains separate schools for boys and girls at the precollege level, and women are not allowed to drive cars, which may change however, as more women are being allowed to enter the workforce. Alcohol consumption is prohibited, public floggings, amputations for those who steal, and even executions are mandatory for crimes ranging from harassment of women, to robbery, homosexuality, adultery, or murder.

Because Osama bin Laden and the 19 terrorists that brought down the twin towers in New York on that fateful day in September, 2001 were raised in Wahhabism, it is not a far reach to see that Osama and the Taliban placed King Abdullah in an awkward position, especially since a large segment of the Saudi population opposed the U.S. policy in the Middle East of total support of Israel against the Palestinians. And the question still exists as to what the Government of Saudi Arabia knew about 9/11 before it happened.

Although the Saudis ended recognition of the Taliban as the legitimate government of Afghanistan, the presence of 5,000 U.S. soldiers stationed on "sacred Islamic soil" in 1990 made bin Laden's appeal to the people of America a symbol of "Muslim defiance against American 'arrogance,' and popularized the 19 Saudis who gave their lives – not for 72 maidens, but rather to strike back for centuries of perceived injustices including the West's desire to control Arab Oil. Thus, the answer to my student's question must be reduced to the perceived injustices of the modern era, which began during WWI, and continued during the British and French occupation of the Mandate System with the open shame of kicking Muslims off the Land, while negating promises and grabbing Arab Oil.

PALESTINE BEFORE ZIONISM

In Jewish consciousness, the term Zionism refers to the belief that the Land of Israel was given to them by God way back at the beginning of their national experience and its founding under Moses its first national leader. Ironically, all of this history is recounted nowhere else from its beginning than in Torah, the Holy Scriptures and known to westerners as the Pentateuch of the Holy Bible. For more than a thousand years, faithful scribes of both Israel and Judah recorded this history throughout the centuries of its existence, subjugation, and occupation.

All of this is fine except that almost all Americans immediately demonstrate ignorance of the other ten tribes of their progenitor Jacob, the grandson of Abraham its ancestor of record. They conveniently forget that the appellation "the Jews" only came about after Solomon's son Rehoboam divided the Kingdom of Israel in I Kings 12: 19, 20 by making a bad political decision. The faithful Israelite scribes recorded the history of Israel's division in I Kings 11: 1 – 13 with the punishment of Rehoboam by God, which would leave him with one tribe (v. 13) consisting of the two Southern tribes – Judah and Benjamin. In addition, and more so connected to the present conflict under study, not only were the ten scattered tribes, descendants of Abraham and Jacob, but there were also the progeny of Abraham's first son, Ishmael, who the world knows as Arabs. Not only do these have a legal right to the Land of Israel; but Moses taught instructions directly from Israel's God that:

"If a man have two wives, one beloved and the other hated, and if they have both borne him children, both the beloved and the hated, and if the firstborn son be hers that was hated; then it shall be, when he maketh his sons to inherit that which he hath, that he may not make the son of the beloved the firstborn before the son of the hated, which is indeed the firstborn: But he shall acknowledge the son of the hated for the firstborn, by giving him a double portion of all that he hath: for he is the beginning of his strength; the right of the firstborn is his." Deut. 21: 15 – 17.

To disavow this scripture in Torah or the Christian's Holy Bible, Jews would have to destroy their holy writings, disavow the Prophet Moses, and deny their God YHWH. As far as the Arab – Muslims are concerned, the descendants of Ishmael are entitled to two-thirds of the Land of Palestine by the Jewish Book, and no less according to Jehovah's own instructions to Moses. Thus, at best, no matter what Israeli hard-liners say, no matter what law the Knesset passes or how many walls they build, no matter what Americans on the Far-Right posit, the truth is that there can be now no settlement without a two-state solution. And that ends that.

In 2009 Moshe Maor wrote an article on the History of Zionism and went to great lengths to make a case for the radical revolution by which the Zionists sought to carve out a Jewish identity. He wrote: "Zionism's revolutionary character stemmed from its emphasis on the need to construct a Jewish national life in response to modernity and to do so only in Eretz Israel — the Land of Israel. Additionally, Zionists were the first to believe that policies on the major issues confronting Jewry should be subject to free and open debate. Furthermore, due to the catastrophic condition of East European Jewry, they were the first to assert that the solution to the "Jewish Problem" hinged on migration to a homeland (Vital, 1998, p. 208-9)."

Citing other authors of the twentieth century, Maor posited that "Zionism provides a classic example of the role of nationalism in the reconstruction of nations." Do these words mirror the 100-year-old fight in which Palestinians and Muslim Arabs have been engaged in their struggle for a national identity and a homeland? While the West and their European friends are quick to render weapons, money, and political as well as socio-cultural support to the Zionists, they systematically, and without shame deny the same or similar rights to those who were descended from the same forefather (according to His Majesty's Government in 1915) but who also lived for centuries on the very same land. Surely, both Maor and Vital were correct in saying that the solution to the Jewish problem hinged on a homeland. However, by the same standard or reasoning, and in similar fashion, historians and truth-seekers of integrity also say today that the solution to the Palestinian problem hinges on the establishment of a national homeland and an established identity. Unfortunately, this historian posits that such a solution will never be reached until Great Britain in humility acknowledges the deliberate deception with which it buried Arab hopes of a recognized identity because of its Secret Agreement to support French colonial goals.

Leo Trepp (1913 – 2010), former professor of Jewish studies at the University of Mainz, Germany, in his book Judaism: Development & Life, recorded a speech by the late Richard Cardinal Cushing of Boston in 1969 which acknowledged that the State of Israel is a "fulfillment of [biblical] prophecy and not just a refuge for people of the world." Trepp admitted that while he accepted Cardinal Cushing's words, he was "cognizant of the sufferings of the Palestinians and empathetic with their aspirations," and begged his readers for their "understanding and forbearance" of his ambivalence between Jewish emotions and denied Palestinian rights (p, 159).

Before we can understand the pain in his conscience as a truth-seeker, we need to examine a little more closely some of the history of Palestine before the onset of modern Zionism.

By the late 1800's, the world was moving toward nationalism, which fueled anti-Semitism. Coincidental to this movement, Charles Darwin had just before in 1859 published his book entitled On Species in which the strong survives. Thus, as this movement of nationalism spread across Europe, Jews everywhere were persecuted more and more, and they fled to Muslim lands for protection. The untold irony of which the world seems ignorant is that in the Jewish Torah, both Jews and Muslims are descended from Shem. Thus, they are both Semitic peoples. This makes Speaker Paul Ryan's recent comment in Congress oxymoronic when he referred to violence against Jews as "anti-Semitic" while violence against Muslims are 'just' "anti-Muslim." The truth of history and ancestry demands that violence against both groups of people be labeled anti-Semitic, and the one is not to be sympathized more than the other. Consequently, Leo Trepp's conscience smarted when he considered that Palestinian refugees were then (and still are in 2017) living in muddy disease-ridden camps in Jordan and elsewhere while Jews from America and the diaspora live comfortably in homes built by those same Palestinians and their ancestors.

History records that Jews had always fled to Muslim lands when European Christians persecuted them. Thus, when they were expelled by Ferdinand and Isabella from Spain in 1492 they fled to the caliphate in Egypt led by Maimonides, the premiere Jewish authoritarian. The Muslims received the preeminent astronomer and physician of Cordova, and allowed him the freedom to write his fourteen-volume *Mishneh Torah* and codify Talmudic law. Maimonides was revered by both Islamic and Jewish scholars, and soon became a prominent figure in Egypt who influenced both the Jewish and Islamic worlds. The Western world needs to know that for centuries Jews and Muslims as well as both cultures thrived as they lived side-by-side. From where, then, does this modern hatred of religion and politics emanate? What modern cause or sociopolitical occurrences were there that brought on such abject hatred and egregious terror, which American College Freshmen cannot understand? To quote one student: "Why are they fighting?" Suffice it to say that the disdain of the West coupled with its military might against rioters seeking justice turned a branch of freedom fighters into radical terrorists who vow to get even. The great irony is that this branch of "Radical Islam" as Donald Trump labels it was spawned by the Wahhabi doctrine of Saudi Arabia – the country to which he now travels in triumph.

If we return to the Edict of 1492 proclaimed by Ferdinand and Isabella, it expelled the Jews from Spain and prohibited them from ever settling in Spain. Thus, Jew and Arabs lived side by side in Palestine since the fifteenth century, and their cultures flourished as Maimonides influenced scholars from both cultures. But although Muslims of the Turkish Empire held possession of the entire region including Saudi Arabia, Syria, Iraq, and Jordan, and even though both Jews and Arabs lived in the land, none held sovereignty at any time. Both Arabs and Jews many years later lived in poverty, and both peoples were supported by their people in diaspora.

Five hundred years ago in 1517, Martin Luther (1483 – 1546), acknowledged widely as the man who started the Protestant Reformation nailed his 95 theses to the door of the church in Wittenberg, Germany. Luther was a man of great contradiction. In 1523, he wrote in the spirit of the times a pamphlet "Jesus Christ Was a Jew" which said that if Jews were treated more kindly by Christians, they may convert and be brought into the fold.

Trepp records Luther's words: "I hope that if Jews are treated in a friendly fashion and instructed from Holy Writ, many of them will become worthy Christians." (79) At first, like Mohammed, the man whom Jewish tribes had honored as "the" mediator between their tribal disputes, Luther expected Jews to flock to his movement, especially since he had worked to purify Christianity from the errors of Roman Catholicism. Like Mohammed, who was bent on purifying Christians and Jews from their unethical behaviors and lax worship of the Creator, Luther, in similar fashion, had engaged on a course to purify the church from its profligate and atrocious activity. And just as Muslims at war told their enemies "convert or die," so Luther wrote a pamphlet later on in 1546 entitled "Of the Jews and Their Lies." In it, he turned viciously against Jews, and admonished the German princes to "expel the hardened blasphemers." He wrote that Christians should burn their synagogues, destroy their houses, and take their prayer books and the books of the Talmud. He further advocated that young Jews be given hoes and mallets and be compelled to earn their bread by the sweat of their brow. He wrote: "Let us follow the example of the people of France, Spain, and Bohemia and "expel them from our land forever." (Trepp 80)

Then, one hundred years later, in 1655 after Oliver Cromwell and Puritan rule deposed King Charles I of England and executed him, Cromwell became convinced that Christ (the Messiah) would not return until the Jews were dispersed all over the world. With that thought, he opened negotiations with Manasseh ben Israel, a Dutch Rabbi, which led to the formal declaration by Parliament that "there was nothing in English law preventing Jewish settlement on English soil." This was the beginning of modern Jewish community in Great Britain (Trepp, 81).

Two hundred years later, as the persecution in Europe began again anew, Jews fled to Palestine hoping that the Arabs would welcome them, as they sought to carve out a better life for both ethnicities – all Semites. History records that in the late 1870s Jews again fled to Muslim Lands. At that time, French Baron Rothschild established colonies in Palestine for the new refugees from Europe. But while the rank and file of Palestinian Islam accepted the new immigrants, the Turkish government which controlled Palestine at that time had no desire for the huge number of non-Muslim immigrants flooding into their empire. Christian immigrants had given them much trouble before, and they now desired an experienced Jewish leader like Maimonides to keep things in order. That leader turned out to be Theodor Herzl (1860 – 1904), who proposed that Jews needed a political solution for their continued problems. He argued that if all Jews would leave their diaspora countries, anti-Semitism would cease, they would be able to develop their spiritual and cultural gifts to the benefit of humanity, while at the same time making them no longer a minority but a people with political capital.

Herzl was born in Budapest and raised as a citizen of the Austrian-Hungarian Empire. He became a novelist and a newspaper correspondent. In 1894, he was assigned to cover the trial of Alfred Dreyfus, a Jewish captain who was the only Jew in the French general staff. Dreyfus had been accused of giving secret documents to the Germans. The German emperor knew the identity of the traitor and that Dreyfus was innocent. However, because he was a Jew, Dreyfus was made the scapegoat and placed on trial for his life. He was convicted and sentenced to Devil's Island. Twelve years later in 1906 he was exonerated through the efforts of Georges Clemenceau future French Prime Minister. In the meantime, Dreyfus' trial convinced Herzl that unless the Jews had their own homeland no Jew was safe anywhere. Thus, Zionism was born, and in 1896 Herzl wrote a brochure, Der Judenstaat, "The Jewish State," in which he argued for a political homeland. Consequently, in 1897 Herzl organized a Jewish Congress in Basel, Switzerland, which was to create a Jewish State, "an internationally recognized homeland in Palestine." (Trepp, 161)

Working alone and facing great obstacles, Herzl had to convince Jews in Europe and America that his plan was not only feasible but possible. He was backed by no government and was the sole representative of a homeless oppressed people. He died at the age of forty-four, which was exactly forty-four years before his dream became a reality when Israel became a state in 1948. Left to carry on his work were Chaim Weizmann, a chemist living in England who had been born in Russia, and later became the first president of the State of Israel, and Louis Brandeis (1856 – 1941), Associate Justice of the U. S. Supreme Court, who became famous as "the" advocate of human rights in America, and friend of oppressed African Americans. However, this does not explain 'Radical Islamic Terrorism' or answer the student's question about why are they fighting? Nor does this history of Zionism tell the story of Palestinian desperation, Arab anger at being deliberately deceived, or the shame of Western disdain and denial of Arab right to a homeland in the one place such territorial claims were to be adjudicated according to Wilson's principle of self-determination – the League of Nations.

The Roots of Arab Bitterness

As nationalism spread across Europe at the beginning of the twentieth century, European nations began to make alliances in the event of war. In August 1914, as though in response to a divine prediction, the guns of August unleashed the horrors of World War I. In July, Franz Ferdinand of Austria and his pregnant wife had toured Sarajevo, Bosnia as a prelude to the annexation of Bosnia and Serbia by the Austrian-Hungarian Empire. In opposition to this idea of annexation members of a militant resistance known as the Black Hand stationed would-be assassins along the route of the motorcade for the express purpose of killing the soon to be King of Austria. The first assassin failed in the attempt when his gun misfired and he was beaten to death by the crowd of on-lookers; but the second militant was successful in carrying out the mission. Austria declared war immediately, and began to mobilize its army.

The Serbs, who were southern Slavs and more desirous of being ruled by their cousins who were northern Slavs, appealed to Russia for help. But as the slow Russian machine took a long time to mobilize, Germany quickly answered the call of its ally Austria. Consequently, Russia's new ally France that had been fighting off and on for 200 years with its neighbor joined the fight against Germany to solidify their alliance with Russia. This also brought France's ally Britain into the conflict. To balance the conflict as a counter-weight, Germany's ally Turkey, which had inherited the old Ottoman Empire, joined the war on the side of Austria, and "as the world turned in 1914" it was at war, with the lesser countries choosing sides.

The only major power that had not yet entered the war in 1914 was the United States of America. Nestled securely between two great oceans, the United States had developed a political strategy of non-intervention because of the last wish of its first president George Washington. More importantly, however, because America was a land of immigrants, there were riots in the streets as Irish-Americans prayed that Germany would punish Great Britain for keeping them in 600 years of slavery in their own land, which misery had forced them to migrate just in order to eat. English and French people in America hoped that the U.S. would join their brothers and cousins in the war so as to defeat the Germans. On the other hand, German Americans and people from Eastern Europe sought to influence the United States to fight on the side of Germany in order to give France the thrashing they deserved for slights going way back to the time of Louis XVI, who had built two cities in Germany and taken over German mines in the Saar Valley for the profits of

French noblemen. France's ambassador to Prussia had also interfered in German-Prussian relations, who were cousins somewhat, and this unforgiveable slight had led to the Franco German War of 1870. The French, still smarting over the Treaty by which France was forced to cede Alsace Lorraine to the Germans, were determined to bring the two-hundred-year-old conflict to an end. So ethnic immigrants in the U.S. fought each other in the streets of America, and President Woodrow Wilson had to tour the country for more than a year trying to bring peace – and, in the process, keep America out of the war.

With the war going badly in 1915 for the Triple Entente, the British entered stage left, so to speak, with an idea that gave rise to the Arab root of bitterness against the West. Charles Smith described the situation in his history Palestine and the Arab-Israeli Conflict. In it he said: "Despite the fact that Britain, France, and Russia were allies who mistrusted each other's motives, their fear of their common enemy was greater than their fear of each other." Germany had embarked on a massive industrial and military expansion since the 1880s and was aggressively involved in the race for colonies, which had raised a general alarm (Smith, 39).

In addition, Germany had gained many concessions from the Ottoman Empire before its collapse, which included most significantly a proposed railway from Constantinople through Baghdad to Basra and the Persian Gulf. As I have written elsewhere, Britain had been sitting in southern Iraq before the 1840s, so I gladly cite Smith's description where "British officials considered southern Iraq a sphere of military and commercial influence, as well as part of a defense perimeter protecting allies in the Gulf and the oil fields discovered in southwest Iran in 1907. Britain controlled these fields, which were vital to its military position in Europe as well as Asia." (59)

To add more fuel to the fire, students should be told that sometime around 1910 Rear Admiral Sir Edmund Slade convinced the British Admiralty that Britain should send oil explorers around the world, and when they found it make deals to acquire control, and use that oil for their commercial interests, while hoarding the oil of their own colonies for war. Thus, in 1911 British geologists searched the provinces of Mesopotamia (Mosul and Basra) for oil while they masqueraded as archaeologists. Then in 1912 with the discovery of oil in Mosul, the Turkish Petroleum Company (TPC) formed in 1911 was used to market the oil.

In March 1914, the TPC was reorganized, and both British and German bankers, and British and German executives sat next to each other with

British and Dutch Oil company representatives who had been invited to London to sit around the conference table. However, notwithstanding the name of the company, Turkey had not been invited to the meeting. Even though the war had not broken out yet, the arguments were hot; and these same issues would continue between Britain and France after the war ended in 1919. Thus, Britain had a distinct motive to deceive the Arabs while seeking a way to aid France in its commercial interests – and all because of Arab Oil.

British Guarantees in McMahon Letters

The question now is: "How did it come about?" After fighting a losing battle from August of 1914, and unable to cajole America into the war, the British approached the Arab caliphate in Egypt led by Sharif Husain in October 1915 with guarantees of Arab independent democracies throughout the Fertile Crescent if they would enter the war against Turkey to even the playing field. Surely British motives were not pure, because they had their eyes on Iraqi Oil, but if they had kept their promises to the Arabs perhaps Islamic terrorists would not have a reason to fight. Here then, is another reason my students would have to process into the equation in order to answer the question before us: "Why are they fighting?"

For several months between July 1915 and January 1916, British High Commissioner in Egypt, Sir Henry McMahon, on the advice of the His Majesty's Government, wrote four (4) letters of negotiation promising independent statehood for all Arab groups if the Arabs would fight against Turkey. But while they made certain promises to the Islamic leader, they also sought economic benefits for their help in advising them in the desire to establish independent Arab democracies. These letters "illustrate Arab requests for independence, to be backed by Britain, and Arab opposition to French territorial claims after the war. On the British side, McMahon strived to leave room for French interests without specifying what they might be and to gain Arab agreement to take action against the Turks." (Smith, 96)

On July 14, 1915, Husain's son Abdullah wished to assure the British Government that his people's interests were "bound to those of your government." He wrote moreover: "Do not trouble to send aero planes or warships to distribute news and reports as in the past." Apparently, the British had engaged in previous propaganda efforts.

In a lengthy statement of condition, Sharif Husain set forth the Arab positions. He wrote that it was the Arab nation's determination to "assert its right to live, gain its freedom and administer its own affairs in name and in fact; and whereas the Arabs believe it to be in Great Britain's interest to lend them assurance and support in the fulfillment of their steadfast and legitimate aims to the exclusion of all other aims; and whereas . . . [they] prefer British assistance to any other . . . . Great Britain recognizes the independence of the Arab countries (boundaries clearly laid out from Persia on the East, the Indian Ocean on the South, the Red Sea and the Mediterranean on the West), Great Britain will agree to the proclamation of an Arab Caliphate for Islam, the Sharifian Arab

Government would grant Great Britain preference in all economic enterprises in the Arab countries; and Great Britain agrees to the abolition of Capitulations in the Arab countries, and undertakes to assist the Sharifian Government in summoning an international congress to decree their abolition."

From the text of the Husain-McMahon Correspondence of 191516 we can analyze the thoughts and feelings of both the Arabs and the British, which are fundamental to the Palestinian-Israeli dispute. In his reply Sir Henry agreed to everything except as to "the question of frontiers and boundaries, [which] negotiations would appear to be premature and a waste of time on details at this stage, with the War in progress and the Turks in effective occupation of the greater part of those regions." Furthermore, he added that " a party of Arabs inhabiting those very regions have, to our amazement and sorrow, overlooked and neglected this valuable and incomparable opportunity, and, instead of coming to our aid, have lent their assistance to the Germans and the Turks . . ." (Smith, 97,98)

In his second letter, Sir Henry agreed to the Arab requests except for two issues: (1) denial of boundary limits for those districts which were not purely Arab namely: Mersin, Alexandretta, portions of Syria lying to the west of the districts of Damascus, Homs, Hama, and Aleppo; and (2) the need to set up special administrative arrangements to protect the two vilayets of Baghdad and Basra "from foreign aggression, to promote the welfare of their inhabitants, and to safeguard our mutual economic interests." At a glance, now that students know some of the rest of the story given above, the British were clearly being deceptive as it sought to hold out territory and situations for their ally France, while they protected their claim and right to Arab Oil discovered in Mosul in 1912. Sir Henry ended the communications by stressing that this "declaration will convince you, beyond all doubt, of great Britain's sympathy with the aspirations of her friends the Arabs; and that it will result in a lasting and solid alliance with them . . .." (99)

In his third correspondence, Sharif Husain argued that "in order to facilitate agreement and serve the cause of Islam . . . we no longer insist on the inclusion of the districts of Mersin and Adana in the Arab Kingdom. As for the vilayets of Aleppo and Bairut and their western maritime coasts, these are purely Arab provinces in which the Moslem is indistinguishable from the Christian, for they are both descendants of one forefather. Since the provinces of Iraq were part of the former Arab Empire, . . .we should find it impossible to . . . renounce the honourable association . . . [but] we should be willing in our desire to facilitate agreement, to allow those parts which are now occupied by

British troops to remain so occupied for a period to be determined by negotiation." (100)

In his third letter dated December 13, 1915, Sir Henry introduces the silent white elephant in the room, so to speak. "I was glad to find that you consent to the exclusion of the vilayets of Mersin and Adana from the boundaries of the Arab countries. . . . As for the two vilayets of Aleppo and Bairut, the Government of Great Britain have fully understood your statement in that respect and noted it with the greatest care. But as [far as] the interests of their ally France are involved in those two provinces, the question calls for careful consideration. We shall communicate again with you on this subject, at the appropriate time." Having mentioned France and her "interests" in land populated in the majority by Arabs, Sir Henry very skillfully ended his note as only a career British diplomat could. He wrote: "In these circumstances, the Government of Great Britain have authorized me to declare to your Lordship that you may rest confident that Great Britain does not intend to conclude any peace whatsoever, of which the freedom of the Arab peoples and their liberation from German and Turkish domination do not form an essential condition."

As one reads Sharif Husain's Fourth Response to Sir Henry McMahon, one senses how the Arab leader must have struggled to remain civil and respectful

even though he is now beginning to understand that Britain is negotiating with a hidden agenda. He replies: "With regard to the northern parts and their coastal regions . . . we have felt bound to steer clear of that which might have impaired the alliance between Great Britain and France . . . [But] on the other hand . . . we shall deem it our duty . . . to claim from you Bairut and its coastal regions which we will overlook for the moment on account of France. Any concession designed to give France or any other Power possession of a single square foot of territory in those parts is quite out of the question. In proclaiming this, I place all my reliance on the declarations which concluded your note, and this reliance is such that, at our death, it shall be inherited by those who live after us. . . ." (Document 3.1, The Husain-McMahon Correspondence July 1915 – January 1916 in Smith, pp.
96 – 101)

The Sykes – Picot Secret Agreement

In order to avoid confusion in terminology, dates, and boundary locations as recorded by some scholars, as a history teacher I offer below the complete text of the Agreement as found in the Jewish Virtual Library on the internet in the public sphere, which was according to Jewish understanding and authentication. Students need to understand what happened in the Sykes-Picot Agreement and they need to answer the question as to whether the Arabs were present or not present, as some later right-wingers appear to want to indicate. Consider this: "If the Arabs were represented historians could not label the Agreement "Secret."

Text of the Sykes-Picot Secret Agreement (Jewish Virtual Library)

"It is accordingly understood between the French and British governments:

That France and Great Britain are prepared to recognize and protect an independent Arab state or a confederation of Arab states (a) and (b) marked on the annexed map, under the suzerainty of an Arab chief. That in area (a) France, and in area (b) Great Britain, shall have priority of right of enterprise and local loans. That in area (a) France, and in area (b)

Great Britain, shall alone supply advisers or foreign functionaries at the request of the Arab state or confederation of Arab states.

That in the blue area France, and in the red area great Britain, shall be allowed to establish such direct or indirect administration or control as they desire and as they may think fit to arrange with the Arab state or confederation of Arab states.

That in the brown area there shall be established an international administration, the form of which is to be decided upon after consultation with Russia, and subsequently in consultation with the other allies, and the representatives of the Shariff of Mecca.

That Great Britain be accorded (1) the ports of Haifa and acre, (2) guarantee of a given supply of water from the Tigres and Euphrates in area (a) for area (b). His Majesty's Government, on their part, undertake that they will at no time enter into negotiations for the cession of Cyprus to any third power without the previous consent of the French government.

That Alexandretta shall be a free port as regards the trade of the British empire, and that there shall be no discrimination in port charges or facilities as regards British shipping and British goods; that there shall be freedom of transit for British goods through

Alexandretta and by railway through the blue area, or (b) area, or area (a); and there shall be no discrimination, direct or indirect, against British goods on any railway or against British goods or ships at any port serving the areas mentioned.

That Haifa shall be a free port as regards the trade of France, her dominions and protectorates, and there shall be no discrimination in port charges or facilities as regards French shipping and French goods. There shall be freedom of transit for French goods through Haifa and by the British railway through the brown area, whether those goods are intended for or originate in the blue area, area (a), or area (b), and there shall be no discrimination, direct or indirect, against French goods on any railway, or against French goods or ships at any port serving the areas mentioned.

That in area (a) the Baghdad railway shall not be extended southwards beyond Mosul, and in area (b) northwards beyond Samarra, until a railway connecting Baghdad and Aleppo via the Euphrates valley has been completed, and then only with the concurrence of the two governments.

That great Britain has the right to build, administer, and be sole owner of a railway connecting Haifa with area (b), and shall have a perpetual right to transport troops along such a line at all times. It is to be understood by both governments that this railway is to facilitate the connection of Baghdad with Haifa by rail, and it is further understood that, if the engineering difficulties and expense entailed by keeping this connecting line in the brown area only make the project unfeasible, that the French government shall be prepared to consider that the line in question may also traverse the Polgon Banias Keys Marib Salkhad tell Otsda Mesmie before reaching area

For a period of twenty years the existing Turkish customs tariff shall remain in force throughout the whole of the blue and red areas, as well as in areas (a) and (b), and no increase in the rates of duty or conversions from ad valorem to specific rates shall be made except by agreement between the two powers.

There shall be no interior customs barriers between any of the above-mentioned areas. The customs duties leviable on goods destined for the interior shall be collected at the port of entry and handed over to the administration of the area of destination.

It shall be agreed that the French government will at no time enter into any negotiations for the cession of their rights and will not cede such rights in the blue area to any third power, except the Arab state or confederation of Arab states, without the previous agreement of his majesty's government, who, on their part, will give a similar undertaking to the French government regarding the red area.

The British and French government, as the protectors of the Arab state, shall agree that they will not themselves acquire and will not consent to a third power acquiring territorial possessions in the Arabian Peninsula, nor consent to a third power installing a naval base either on the east coast, or on the islands, of the red sea. This, however, shall not prevent such adjustment of the Aden frontier as may be necessary in consequence of recent Turkish aggression.
The negotiations with the Arabs as to the boundaries of the Arab states shall be continued through the same channel as heretofore on behalf of the two powers.

It is agreed that measures to control the importation of arms into the Arab territories will be considered by the two governments.

I have further the honor to state that, in order to make the agreement complete, his majesty's government [is] proposing to the Russian government to exchange notes analogous to those exchanged by the latter and your excellency's government on the 26th April last. Copies of these notes will be communicated to your excellency as soon as exchanged. I would also venture to remind your excellency that the conclusion of the present agreement raises, for practical consideration, the question of claims of Italy to a share in any partition or rearrangement of turkey in Asia, as formulated in Article 9 of the agreement of the 26th April 1915, between Italy and the allies.

His Majesty's Government further considers that the Japanese government should be informed of the arrangements now concluded."

Sources: Encyclopedia Judaica. © 2008 The Gale Group. All Rights Reserved.

On November 23, 1915, a British delegation led by Sir Arthur Nicolson opened the first round of discussions in London with the French Government represented by Francois-Georges Picot, a professional diplomat with extensive experience in the Levant. Four weeks later a second round of discussions was held with Sir Mark Sykes, an expert on the Middle East, leading the British delegation. The terms of the partition of the old Ottoman Empire inherited by Turkey and Germany were agreed to and signed on May 23, 1916.

Any reader who desires to do more research or to see the areas mentioned in the Sykes-Picot secret Agreement document could find a map published by the Encyclopedia Britannica Media, which shows the areas referred to above. Britain and France were determined to divide up German holdings at the end of the war. the economic benefits of those areas were to accrue to them.

But what about the Arabs? In the first place, the agreement was a complete violation of the terms already agreed to between the Arabs and Great Britain and the understanding given to Sharif Husain of Mecca. On his part, he was supposed to convince the Arabs to join Great Britain in the fight against Turkey; but according to the correspondence with Sir Henry the previous year, the Arabs would eventually receive much more than what was being partitioned out to them by Britain and France, with Russian agreement.

Secondly, readers should notice the part which says: "It is agreed that measures to control the importation of arms into the Arab territories will be considered by the two governments." Why control the importation of arms into the Arab territories; but give the Jews more than needed – even the nuclear weapons which the world now knows that Israel has possessed for decades? Why would Palestinians and Arabs agree to this provision? And how could Britain and France think that the Arabs would agree to this provision even after Sharif Husain Fourth Letter to Sir Henry McMahon clearly repudiated the thought of "a single square foot of territory" being given to

France or any other Power? Therefore students, who are seeking to know the truth of the present conflict and its origin, need to ask two more questions also: (a) "Why are teenage boys fighting with stones in the streets against tanks and heavy armaments"; and (b) "Why would elderly women, even some who have children, strap on vests with bombs and blow themselves up in restaurants and public buses? Do they embrace death just to go to Paradise and be given 72 virgins? Or are they fighting in Palestine for what they perceive to be God-given Rights according to the Jewish Torah?" (Deuteronomy 21: 15 – 17) Common reason and logical thinking should reveal that the politicians and leaders of western governments are far from being honest about the root cause of Arab bitterness; but they find it easy and more manipulative to throw out declarations against "Islamic Terrorism." No wonder Trepp, a good Jew like many others, found his conscience disturbed and rapt in much conflict.

In the third place, this secret agreement created more confusion by causing Italy to make claims. The Agreement was communicated in August 1916 to Italy after they declared war against Germany, and Italy now hoped to get a piece of the pie and a sphere of influence. Thus, in April 1917, Britain and France in the Agreement of Saint Jean-de-Maurienne promised Southern and South-West Anatolia to

Italy, which also violated the Husain-McMahon contract.

No doubt a Righteous God wanted to expose the skullduggery (to use a well-known British phrase) so He allowed the Bolshevik Revolution to remove the Czar of Russia and expose the Secret Agreement to the world in late 1917. The United States, which had just entered the war was embarrassed, the new Russian government was vindicated, and the overjoyed Turks celebrated. The subsequent withdrawal of Russia from the war cancelled the Russian aspect of the Sykes-Picot Agreement, and Turkey's ongoing victories led to the gradual abandonment of the Anatolia provision. The Arabs, who only learned about the Sykes-Picot Secret Agreement to divide up its lands when the Bolsheviks published it in late 1917 were scandalized. Their resentment against Great Britain and the West grew and became magnified despite the modifications made by Great Britain, and the nullification of the document by the Allied Conference of San Remo, Italy in April 1920 did nothing to appease them.

History demands that all students everywhere recognize that this event perpetrated by the British and French in 1916 was the first cause of the Arab Uprising of the 1920s, which got worse in the 1930s despite Britain's installation of the Grand Mufti.

Although hand-picked by Britain, Amin al-Husseini, the Grand Mufti was at first an advocate for the local nationalism of Palestinian Arabs, who as early as 1920 actively opposed Zionism and was sentenced to ten years in prison for citing the Nebi Musa riots of 1920. In 1921, the British High Commissioner pardoned him and appointed him Grand Mufti of Jerusalem in the hope that he could quell the Arab riots. While he worked for the British agenda, however, he still promoted Arab nationalism against Zionism. During the 1936 – 39 Arab revolt in Palestine he fled to the French Mandate of Lebanon to avoid arrest by the British, and remained antagonistic to them until his death in 1974. During WWII, al-Husseini declared support for Hitler, as did the Vatican. Both of them supported Hitler in his persecution of Jews. Thus, Britain continued to make extremely bad decisions trying to evade confession of what it had done, and continued to show disdain for the Arab people by its policies. Thus, resentment got worse during the years of its Mandate causing Muslim anger against the West to grow.

The Secret Agreement between Britain and France was officially abrogated by the Allies at the San Remo Conference in April 1920, but it was quickly replaced by the Mandate for Palestine, which the League of Nations led by Britain conferred upon Great Britain. Where was the United States in 1920?

History reveals that the so-called brains of America – the Republican Senators who wanted to win an election, and had agreed between themselves to deny anything Woodrow Wilson the Democrat had done – had removed the only world power capable of steering a just and righteous cause in this escalating debacle from the world's stage, which left Great Britain as the Big Dog in the fight supported by France.

On September 11, 2001 the student asked: "Why are they fighting"? If you have read this far, perhaps now you can give a better answer to the question, which may help the war-hawks of America. Perhaps now you can tell President Trump that the continued slights of Great Britain, coupled with America's perceived compliance, had pushed the legitimate resentment of militant Wahhabi Muslims of Saudi Arabia down the scale toward revenge for the West's Arab Land grab, but which will yet burst forth after 1948 into what Dick Cheney and George Bush called "terrorism" – after a few more years of negated guarantees. Thus, at this point, the stage is set for a fight to begin; but not yet – not until after 1948.

Balfour Declaration & Zionist Homeland

During the first two years of the war, the British Government had very little concern for the strategic value of Palestine. For them, its main value was seen as a buffer zone between French-controlled Lebanon and Syria and the British-controlled Egypt. Then Mark Sykes suggested that Britain should reserve Haifa and Acre on the coast for British suzerainty, and push for the internationalization of Palestine. But even though Zionists in London began to urge support for a Jewish homeland in Palestine, as Smith wrote: "Some, including the Foreign Secretary, Arthur Balfour, wished to hand over authority in Palestine to the United States if internationalization were no longer the accepted procedure." (72) The problem was that America had not yet entered the war.

In May of 1915, the government of Herbert Henry Asquith, First Earl of Oxford and Asquith began to collapse as he and his War Secretary, David Lloyd George quarreled over 'the lack of shells' where the British army was running low on shells due to a serious miscalculation of 'front-line strategy' and the use of shelling to control the battlefield. David Lloyd George, a Conservative who sympathized with the

Zionists push for a homeland, suggested and won approval for a war committee to prosecute the war. Asquith, who was elevated to the House of Lords after winning back his seat ten years later, faded from leadership soon after that and was replaced by Lloyd George who became Prime Minister (See The First World War: Volume I: To Arms by Hew Francis Anthony Strachan – pub. by Oxford Press). Lloyd George immediately began "to involve himself in all aspects of foreign policy, much to the alarm of the Foreign Office" (Smith, 72)

Another crisis emerged in February 1917. Defeats by Germany had brought the Russian army to a state of mutiny. Meanwhile, in Petrograd there was great unrest, and riots signaled that Bolshevik revolutionaries would soon topple the Czar and take control of the Russian government. Concerned that the Russia might withdraw from the war, Lloyd George promoted Zionism as a means of persuading Russian Jews to support Russia's war effort. This idea, however, as Smith recounts, encouraged the "London Zionists to foster official British sentiment for a pro-Zionist declaration, as they were aware that no such Russian Jewish backing for the war effort existed." (72) Thus, on November 2, 1917, British Foreign Secretary Arthur Balfour wrote a letter to Lionel Walter Rothschild, 2nd Baron Rothschild at his home in 148 Piccadilly declaring:

> "His Majesty's Government view with favour the establishment in Palestine of a national home for the Jewish people, and will use their best endeavours to facilitate the achievement of this object, it being clearly understood that nothing shall be done which may prejudice the civil and religious rights of existing non-Jewish communities in Palestine, or the rights and political status enjoyed by Jews in any other country."

The British angle depended upon the hope that their support for Zionism would lead American Jews to pressure President Woodrow Wilson to enter the war on the side of the Entente – Britain, France, and Russia. The gambit worked, and the United States entered the war on April 6, 1917.

The Balfour Declaration of 1917, as it became known, was by all means the haphazard result of political lobbying by Jewish Zionists, and while the text of the official document appears to grant the Palestinians and all "non-Jewish" persons freedom of religion, seriously lacking from the document was any hint that the Palestinian Arabs would be granted "citizenship rights" in this "New" Jewish state. Thus, all Arabs and Muslims everywhere could not perceive any honesty or integrity in the document, and could only view it as a "sell-out" by the British in order to achieve their own selfish ends. To make it worse, thoughts about the proposed law of keeping weapons and arms away from the Palestinians and Arabs ratcheted up to the highest level of resentment all the anger and distrust that a sane person could imagine.

Thus, I boldly ask the reader the student's question: "Why are they fighting?" And again, I ask: "Is it to get 72 maidens in Paradise at death, or could it be because of some other more family-oriented reasons?" Remember that Sharif Husain had made it quite clear that "Any concession . . . to give France or any other Power possession of a single square foot of territory . . . is quite out of the question . . . [and] I place all my reliance on the declarations which concluded your note, and this reliance is such that, at our death, it shall be inherited by those who live after us." Both historians and their students can only interpret this final negotiated plank by Sharif Husain to mean that "at our death, our children and grandchildren will inherit the Independent Arab democracies you promise to help us establish in return for the economic concessions to Arab Oil you requested." (My emphasis) So then, do Palestinian mothers strap on vests and detonate them in order to get 72 maidens or could it possibly be related to the British guarantee of Arab Statehood?

British Mandate & French Occupation

The Mandate System

The Treaty of Versailles, which was signed in January 1919 to end World War I, did more damage to the world than good. Many historians including the writer blame the Republican-controlled U.S. Senate for the political confusion that resulted from the League of Nation's Mandate System. Because Woodrow Wilson, a Democrat, had been hailed as a savior by Europeans primarily because of his Fourteen Points, Republican politicians did not want to give him any credit since 1920 was an election year (they would do the same thing to Barack Obama in 2012). Thus, because they were only concerned about taking political power in 1920, they refused to ratify the Treaty of Versailles or join the League of Nations, which was Wilson's grand solution for maintaining global peace among nations. With America absent from the world's stage, Britain became world leader with its ally France in tow. And with that absence of the United States from the world's stage, American GOP politics would settle on the world's skin like a cancer for the next 25 years.

During WWI, British forces had occupied Iraq, a name they gave Mesopotamia as the war began. Because of their interest in Arab oil, they had worked with Arab tribal leaders to launch a revolt against the sultan who had inherited the crumbling Ottoman Empire. Their promise to help the Arabs form an independent democratic state in return for commercial considerations was the driving force, which prompted Arab officers to join the British in their Iraqi campaign. However, as we now know, the British never kept their promise. They had made other commitments to the French in the Sykes-Picot Secret Agreement of 1916. The most they could do now was to organize protectorates, which they called mandates with the promise of implementing Wilson's Fourteenth Point of self-determination of all peoples. Consequently, with America AWOL, and Great Britain as the leader of the world aided by France, they pushed through the arrangement, which was hurriedly approved by the League of Nations. Iraq, Jordan, Palestine and Egypt became British Mandates, while France controlled Syria, Lebanon, Morocco, and Algiers. King Faisal was hailed as "Protector of the Shrines" but the real power rested with the governments of Britain and France – and the Secret Agreement made between them.

After the signing of the Treaty of Versailles in January 1919, the next 20 years would witness the seething and growth of Arab resentment as fueled by

British negation of the written guarantees given to Husain in 1915, and the Arab understanding of Britain's deliberate deception in 1916 and 1917. The United States, which seemed to do anything the British wanted without regard for the other people in the world, were complicit in British skullduggery only to be awakened by the rise of the Third Reich, and Hitler's repudiation of the Treaty of Versailles.

On the eve of the Paris Peace Conference of 1919, Emir Faisal, acting on behalf of the Arab Kingdom of Hejaz, and Chaim Weizmann, acting on behalf of the Zionist Organization signed an agreement which reflected their mutual interests and goals in Syria and Palestine. Unfortunately, however, no Palestinian Arab view was consulted. The irony is that although the Faisal-Weizmann Agreement recognized the Balfour Declaration of 1917, and agreed that there would be freedom of religion and the exercise thereof for all, and that the Mohammedan Holy Places would be under Mohammedan control, that there would be no religious test for the exercise of civil or political rights, and that all disputes would be arbitrated by the British, the Agreement did not confer citizenship or citizenship rights on the Arabs of Palestine. Emir Faisal did, however, state that if the Arabs did not obtain their independence the document would be deemed null and void. The gorilla in the room would ask the question himself: "Did they gain independence in Palestine?" The truth is that all the

Arabs from Iraq and Palestine were under British Mandate from 1920 while Syria and Lebanon were mandated to French control by the Covenant of the League of Nations in April 1920.

By the time the British turned Palestine over to the Zionists for a Jewish homeland in 1948 and Chaim Weizmann became its first Prime Minister, it became clear to all Arabs and Muslims that the British had reneged on the written guarantees of 1915. They also recognized the disdain in which they were held when Britain had even gone to the League of Nations in 1922 to declare that the peoples of the former Ottoman Empire needed tutelage and development because they were unfit for self-determination.

Thus, Muslims from Iraq to Egypt and especially those of Syria, Lebanon, Palestine, and Algiers now recognized that they had been duped and were not independent and free, but occupied, tortured and dismissed as ignorant by the French. The people of Algiers resisted, and the resistance turned into a revolution, which quickly brought on the military might of the French occupiers in Algiers, and the fight for survival began, which quickly sparked Muslim resentment against the West in modern times. Thus, it is no wonder that in 2003, President George Bush ordered all US military leaders to read watch the movie Battle for Algiers, and try to understand the French occupation against the

Muslims in Algiers, and the response of the people in anticipation of what could be expected in Iraq.

The irony of this history is seen in two points: (1) Torah teaches that the Jewish God (albeit the Christian God and the Muslim Allah) told Moses that the descendants of Abraham's first son Ishmael is entitled to two-thirds of the land; and (2) the British had given its written guarantees to Arab possession of the land before giving it to the Zionists. Also, the Palestinian and Arab Muslims by 1919 felt that they deserved consideration not only for their service during the war, but also because they accommodated Britain's desire for Oil for its armaments and its ships. Besides all this, the internationalization of Muslim sufferings under French occupation and the Mandate System, and the torture suffered by the F.L.N. in their Battle for Algiers. This added another slight that kept resentment growing.

French brutality in Algiers and Morocco of the 1950s bred the young terrorists of Paris 60 years later (2015-17). Algeria's youth who had grown up in France, and considered French by De Gaulle, but who were treated shabbily by French citizenry, were left with a bitter taste which ignited sparks of recent terrorism in the streets of Paris. Thus, while Americans are trained to mouth words like "Radical Islamic Terrorists" none of them are taught the historical background; and they are never taught to ask why Muslim women or Muslim teenage boys would strap bombs to their chest and blow themselves up. Surely they could not all be doing so in order to have sex with 72 maidens in Paradise. Even the rhetoric of western politicians in this regard does not follow a logical pattern of debate; and, from the foregoing, it becomes obvious that no solution to the Palestinian question will materialize until Great Britain openly confesses to its deliberate deception in 1915 and the West confess to its disdain after 1917.

Analysis of the Arab Revolts Since 1922

Iran's Hostage Crisis (1979)

As I have written elsewhere, former President George W. Bush did nothing new by giving control of Basra and the Iraqi Oil Fields to Tony Blair and the British military in 2004, because the British had been salivating over Iranian and Iraqi oil in the Persian Gulf for almost one hundred years, ever since the British navy had upgraded its fleet to oil in 1912. The Iranian reserves had been its source of supply since then. Almost immediately Rear Admiral Sir Edmund Slade had suggested that Britain seek to control as much of the world's oil fields that it could, and the British did just that when oil was discovered in Mosul in 1912. Thus, in 1920 it was too good to be true when the League of Nations Mandate gave Britain control over the very places its government desired to be – the rich oil fields of Iraq and Iran.

In 1953 the British Secret Service planned and launched a coup d'état designed to overthrow the democratically elected government of Prime Minister Mohammed Mosaddegh in order to strengthen the monarchical but dictatorial rule of

Mohammad Reza Pahlavi on the 19th of August 1953. The British Secret Service orchestrated this action under the name "Operation Boot" and coerced the United States Central Intelligence Agency to join them in "Operation Ajax".

After Prime Minister Mosaddegh was elected he tried to audit the Anglo-Iranian Oil Company (AIOC), a British corporation (now the grandfather of British Petroleum). He wanted to limit the British corporation's control over Iran's oil reserves. When the AOIC refused to co-operate with the Iranian government, however, its parliament voted to nationalize the oil industry, and began to expel all foreign corporate representatives from the country. Britain retaliated by calling for a worldwide boycott of Iranian oil in the hopes of bringing Iran to its knees. Initially, the British Government had mobilized the army to seize control of the British built oil refinery, but Prime Minister Clement Attlee opted instead to tighten the economic boycott and use Iranian mafia-type thugs to undermine Mosaddegh's government.

Western Conspiracy Between Britain & CIA

Winston Churchill and the Eisenhower Administration met and conspired to overthrow Mosaddegh's government, even though the Truman Administration had opposed interfering in Iran's sovereignty the year before. Declassified documents reveal that British intelligence officials planned the coup, and that the AIOC contributed $25,000 to bribe Iranian officials and top military officers. Sixty years later, when the documents were released the Central Intelligence Agency (CIA) finally admitted openly that the CIA was in charge of both the planning and the execution of the coup, including the bribing of Iranian politicians, security and high-ranking army officials, as well as distributing pro-coup Goebbels-style propaganda. The CIA admitted that the coup was carried out "under CIA direction" and "as an act of U.S. foreign policy, conceived and approved at the highest levels of government".

After the coup toppled the Mosaddegh Government, a new government was formed which allowed Mohammad-Rezā Shāh Pahlavi, the Shah of Iran to rule – albeit as a CIA puppet. He had to rely heavily on U. S. support to remain in power because the people clearly resented what the West had done. Mohammad-Reza resorted to much brutality until in 1979 the people (mainly students) could no longer keep quiet, and they began to agitate. According to the CIA's declassified documents just as the conspirators had planned, some of the most feared mobsters in Tehran were hired by the CIA to stage pro-Shah riots on 19th of August.

Other CIA-paid men were brought into Tehran in buses and trucks, and took over the streets of the city. Between 200 and 300 people were killed in the conflict. Mosaddegh was arrested, tried and convicted of treason by the Shah's military court. On 21 December 1953, he was sentenced to three years in jail, and placed under house arrest for the remainder of his life. Other Mosaddegh supporters were imprisoned, and several received the death penalty.
After the coup, the Shah continued his rule as monarch for the next 26 years until he was overthrown in the Iranian Revolution of 1979. (See Wikipedia and other internet files to confirm documented accuracy)

At the time, the Iranian students were contemplating action against the Shah, an Islamic religious resurgence flowed across the country, and calls for the return of Ayatollah Khomeini from London were heard everywhere. The religious leader had fled in exile from the Shah, but had continued to write and agitate for an Islamic Religious State. He returned to Iran after the Shah had left for America, and became Supreme Leader of a government based on the teachings of Islam. At his urging, the Iranians stormed the U.S. Embassy in Tehran, took 66 Americans hostage and for 444 days President Jimmy Carter had the Iran Hostage Crisis on his hand.

All American History books vilify the Iranians for storming the U. S. Embassy, kidnapping Americans, and brassily holding them hostage for ransom. But none of them ever told students the background that led to this event. Thus, generations of Americans who read about the Islamic terrorists in Iran that kidnapped Americans grew up without knowing hardly anything about the kidnap and murder of Prime Minister Mohammed Mosaddegh or the British greed for Iranian Oil. Consequently, while students in Iran were fighting for Freedom from a brutal dictator controlled by the CIA, students in the West were taught that students in Iran were actually "radical Islamic terrorists" intent on establishing a caliph and spreading their doctrine throughout the Middle East while manufacturing nuclear weapons to destroy Israel. Thus, because of this untruth, Muslims in Iran had their own reasons for harboring resentment against America and for distrusting anything United States politicians said.

Iraq-Iran War (1980 – 1988)

Shortly afterward the release of the hostages during the Reagan Presidency, the United States felt that if they gave food to Iraq, it would allow them to use their money to buy armaments from Russia and France. Over the years since the Iran – Iraq War

(1980 – 1988), many Americans have asked if the U.S. sold weapons to Iraq. The truth seems to be that the United States actually sold some helicopters to Iraq shortly before Saddam Hussein invaded Iran. But because he was trying to take advantage of the confusion in Iran after the Shah's government fell, Saddam invaded Iran. At first the U.S. displaying its fear of an Islamic Caliphate was willing to arm Saddam and give support against the Ayatollah. Thus, it gave food and allowed Iraq to get weapons from Russia and France. By the time of war's end, however, the United States had given Saddam Hussein more than one billion dollars.

Questions about the U.S.-Iraq-Iran Relationship still abound; and while many people asked: "Did the Reagan Administration sell arms to Saddam Hussein?" they also asked: "Did the U.S. sell arms to Iran?" The answer is yes to both, but in a round-about way. The United States actually asked Israel to supply the arms to Iran, which it did secretly. The Israelis then ordered weapons from the United States, which they paid for later. In addition, by the time the war was more than half-way over Americans were made aware that a scandal was brewing about an Iran-Contra connection. Far from being rumors, Americans heard President Reagan's personal Television acknowledgments on at least two separate occasions, and subsequent notes from Lieutenant

Oliver North's notebook suggested that President Reagan was aware of what was going on.

The Reagan Administration's policy from day one was that the communist regime in Nicaragua had to go. Thus, President Reagan vowed to help the Sandinista rebels by any means necessary. After notes from Oliver North's book were revealed, they seemed to suggest that President Reagan was aware that there was an arms deal-hostage-drug operation in effect. The irony here is that for its own reasons the Reagan Administration's Foreign Policy had it supporting both Iraq and Iran in the eight-year war.

In a televised interview between Alex Chadwick and Mike Shuster, National Public Radio's (NPR) Foreign Correspondent for Diplomatic Policy, Chadwick asked if the Reagan Administration created Saddam Hussein. Shuster gave an eye-opening answer:

"In actuality, Saddam Hussein has created Iraq's secret police and intelligence, and he became the number one strongman of Iraq in 1979. Thus, the United States played a key role in all of his military and political actions in the Middle East because they had chosen Iraq, led by Saddam Hussein, to be its surrogate for policy in the Persian Gulf, and to counter the actions of Iran, which the Reagan Administration perceived to be the biggest threat.

And the fact that it supported Saddam Hussein in all these clandestine ways, a man who had been the pariah to the United States in the decade earlier, it . . . could not have helped more to encourage Saddam's grandiosity about his role in the Arab world. He was meeting with senior US diplomats. They were looking the other way when he was using chemical weapons and developing other unconventional weapons. He couldn't have helped but to think that the United States was behind him." (Conversation between Alex Chadwick and Mike Shuster NPR Foreign correspondent – Diplomatic Policy – [U.S. Links to Saddam Hussein] Wikipedia)

All students who will research the U. S. Relationship to Iraq and Iran during that war will discover that the United States actually gave Saddam the chemical weapons he used to kill the Kurds after they tried to assassinate him. Perhaps this was why President George W. Bush was pushed to take out Saddam Hussein on a rumor that he had weapons of mass destruction. With him gone, no one would be able to prove anything. But the fact that no one in the West said anything at the time when Saddam used the chemical weapons is evidence that he had gotten it from United States companies. Then, the United States made another big mistake. Rather than incorporate the Iraq army into a security force of some kind during the occupation, they disbanded a huge army led by career generals and a trained army staff. No doubt some of these same military men were or are now engaged in ISIS. Instead of being soldiers in a regular army. no doubt many of them, who harbor grudges against the United States, fight now as "terrorists."

Chronological Events for Muslim Resentment

The list of perceived slights of modern times, and the deliberate dishonesty of the West as found in history may be seen in these events and Agreements:

1915 – The McMahon Letters guaranteed Independent Arab Democracies. Britain even went so far as to stress that Britain and no other power would have the right to steer the Arabs in their independent democracies.

1916 – The Sykes-Picot Secret Agreement between Britain and France conspired to divide up all German holdings of the former Ottoman territory between them, and take control of the Oil found in the countries of the Fertile Crescent.

1917 – The Balfour Declaration announces British support for a Jewish Homeland in Palestine. The British completely negated their promise to the Arab

Muslims, and Muslims in all countries resented this move.

1919 – The General Syrian Congress refused to recognize a French Government of Syria and argued for ratification of the original Husain McMahon Declaration of 1915.

1919 – Zionists began to flood into Palestine and agitate for Palestinians to be deported to Syria.

1920 – Covenant of the League of Nations, but the United States refuse to ratify the League and GOP Senators make the US absent from world politics.

1920/1 – May Day Riots. On May Day 1921 Jewish communists paraded through the streets of Tel Aviv in support of a Soviet Palestine. The Arabs opposed them and fights broke out. Fourteen Arabs and forty-three Jews were killed. An Arab delegation comprised of members of "notable families went to London in July 1921, demanding that the Balfour declaration be repudiated and that Britain agree to build an Arab national government. Their claims were rejected by British officials, including Winston Churchill, who offered them a representative assembly with an Arab majority but denied it effective power to block British support of Zionist cause." (Smith, 115-116) This led to a White paper of 1922, in which Britain declared that it did "not contemplate that Palestine as a whole should be converted into a Jewish National home, but that such a home should be founded in Palestine" [See Document 4.1]" (Smith, 116 and 159 for Document 4.1 "The Churchill White Paper").

1920 – The Mandate for Palestine was ratified by the League of Nations led by the British. The Balfour Declaration was approved and incorporated in the British Mandate, and the British pushed for a Jewish Homeland unabated. However, although the British were awarded the Palestine Mandate in April 1920, the League of Nations did not ratify it until July 1922, because the United States Senate controlled by Republicans had refused to ratify the Treaty of Versailles or join the League of Nations in 1920.

1936–1939 Arab Riots Against Jewish-migration. With Hitler's rise to power in 1933, thousands of Jews flooded into Palestine no doubt buoyed by the fact that the Zionists had won for them a national homeland – especially after the 1922 ratification by the League of Nations.

Arab Palestinians immediately protested and rioted against the illegal immigration. Young Jewish toughs met Arab youth who supported a secret society Holy War, and who had begun to amass weapons in preparation for an open armed resistance to British domination. At the bottom of this call for a Holy War was the 20- year deception signed by the British known as the Balfour Declaration, which highlighted the original hidden agenda of Great Britain in 1915.

In 1935 Sheikh Izz ad-Din al-Qassam was killed during a general strike ordered by the British-appointed Grand Mufti of Jerusalem, Mohammad Amin al-Husayni as a protest against the massive illegal Jewish immigration. The strike lasted six months from April to October 1936, which brought on a revolt in two phases. By October, the British had defeated phase one by political concessions and international diplomacy; however, in 1937, they brutally suppressed a peasant-led resistance, which killed almost 3,000 Arabs in the process. Al-Husayni fled to Lebanon to escape arrest.

1939 – White Paper on Jewish Immigration. On May 17, 1939, the British Government issued a White Paper which challenged the idea that Palestine could be a Jewish state in spite of Arab opposition. "The White Paper stipulated that Jewish immigration was to be permitted during the next five years (1939 – 1943) at a rate that would bring Jewish population to a level of approximately one third that of the total population. After this five-year period had elapsed, further Jewish immigration was not to be permitted 'unless the Arabs of Palestine acquiesce to it. (163)" All this White Paper did was exacerbate the perceived slight of broken promises by the British, especially since the White Paper had failed to address the McMahon Guarantees.

1948 – Britain turns over Palestine to the Zionists for a homeland for Jews, even though it had begged the United States to assume control the year before. In 1947, Britain's economy was shot due to a long and protracted World War II. Hitler's bombing of London had produced harsh economic realities on Britain, and it wanted to get rid of its Palestinian headache. But after the war there were as many as 100,000 Jews living in camps in French-controlled territory.
Zionists leaders purchased an old ship from the British Ministry of War Transport and some 4,515 Jews boarded a renamed SS Exodus bound for Palestine with plans of breaking through a British blockade and landing its passengers on the beach. By their stubborn tactics, however, they forced the British to commandeer the ship and sail it back to French territory.

It was perhaps at this time that Britain and America could have allowed these Jews safety in England and America until they worked out a political compromise with the Arabs and establish two independent states. A decision at that moment would have had a much chance of resolving the issue than it does now. The issue had never been about both ethnicities sharing the land, the issue has always been about a national identity for both. Thus, Palestinian resentment surfaced as warlike anger, and many swore revenge against this western betrayal when the British gave possession of the land to the Jews in 1948 to comply with the Balfour Declaration.

1953 – British Secret Service, British Oil Company and the CIA conspired to kidnap and assassinate Iran's Prime Minister Mohammed Mosaddegh because he declared his intention to pass laws which would preserve Iranian Oil for the Iranian people and not Westerners. Britain and the United States launched a *coup* and then installed Mohammed Reza, Shah of Iran as a puppet who continued British Oil concessions. Twenty years of the Shah's brutality led to the occupation of the American Embassy in Tehran by Iranian students who kidnapped 66 American hostages and held them for 444 days seeking negotiation. Once again, Republican Senators seeking political power in the United States requested that the hostages not be released to give then President Jimmy Carter any credit, but wait until after the election to release them for the credit of Ronald Reagan, the Republican candidate.

1969 – Al-Aqsa Mosque Fire. On August 21, 1969 a fire set by Dennis Rohan, an Australian evangelical in the Al – Aqsa Mosque in
Jerusalem destroyed a 1000-year-old historic pulpit donated by Saladin in the 12th Century. To add insult

to injury, Rohan told the court that he was acting as "the Lord's emissary" to hasten the coming of the Messiah, who would burn the mosque anyway.

Although the damage done to the mosque was repaired to some extent by a Jordanian contribution of US$9 million dollars, the seething resentment against the West grew more intensely (Since anything Australian is seen as British and allied to the United States). Furthermore, although Israel denied it, Taissir Rahjab al-Tamimi, Chairman of the Islamic Law High Council of the Palestinian Authority declared in 2004 that Israel conspired with Rohan to burn down the mosque, and Muslims around the world believe it and continue to resent British disdain and American hegemony.

The burning of the Al-Aqsa Mosque in Israeli-occupied Jerusalem brought about the forming of the Organization of the Islamic Conference (OIC), which revived the desire for a universal community with a national identity. At this moment, however, Muslims everywhere decry the failure of the OIC to get Israel to: (a) withdraw from Arab territories captured during the Yom-Kippur War; (b) restore legitimate rights to Palestinians; (c) stop the bulldozing of Palestinian homes; (d) stop the building of a wall all across Palestinian territory; and (e) to get an openly confessed Israeli agreement that the Palestinians have a 'God-given' right to live on the land, according to Moses's instruction in *Torah* (Deut.21:15-17).

While the recitation of these occurrences of history were not meant to disgrace one side or the other, the facts of the history show that the majority of the world's Muslim adherents have legitimate gripes against Britain and the West. The facts also reveal how and why the "radicals" in Islam could push to gain redress for these grievances, and they also seem to direct attention back to the Balfour declaration and Britain's politically motivated White Paper of 1922.

Perhaps if Winston Churchill had acknowledged the truth of both documents, made an open confession of Britain's economic interests, and clearly called for a two-state solution at that time, maybe the Palestinian – Israeli question would have been solved, especially since they are both S(h)emite peoples descended from Shem ibn Noah, Abraham's ancestor. Jews have and have had "radicals" as well as America have had many war-hawks and "radicals" that fill U.S. History books. And no doubt the British saw the Founding Fathers of America as "terrorists" in 1774 – 1777.

Thus, while the history student can get an answer to her question with which she might disagree, the thrust of the matter seems to suggest that the West needs to change its rhetoric, forget the nasty political diatribe, and usher in a deliberate move toward sociocultural understanding among the peoples of the world. This can only be done by direct participation and leadership through the United Nations on the world's stage; but it cannot happen with a stance of making America the only "great' nation in the world. America is already great, because the Creator made it so, and placed it between too wide oceans as a 'safe' place for those running from devilish persecution in the old world. (Prophecy in Revelation 12: 117)

Perhaps students who know the facts know that everyone in America is either an immigrant or descended from an immigrant. Even the Native Americans crossed the icy land bridge at Alaska before it melted some 12 – 14,000 years ago. Thus, if the reader becomes engaged in history, she/he will discover that the world changed in the 1840s, and then changed again dramatically in 1900. Industrialization brought changes again in 1914, in 1945, and again in 1975. Swords were turned into muskets, and muskets into field guns. Field guns became long range artillery by the 1840s. The greed of colonialism and the jingoism of the twentieth century brought on the terrorism of the twenty-first century, which demands better understanding and diplomacy than the senseless political rhetoric of the past.

Consequently, world leaders need to lead because it should be obvious by now that things will never again be the same. And if we are the best, and will be again the greatest, how is it that no-one can make a tree? And if we can make mechanical brains – computers and cell phones, how is it that with all our knowledge we create problems that we cannot solve? Perhaps it is time to stop lying, and time to start living; because until we can put oxygen and gravity between the planets in the cosmos, we need to consider the fact that unseen forces more intelligent than we are still control planetary orbits and weather patterns.

The eighteen-year-old asked "Why do 'they' hate us"? Perhaps now as a 35-year-old mother, she can teach the boys in the house that brothers all bleed the same way, get hungry the same way, get tired the same way, and have love for their families and friends the same way. They will all fight for turf, revenge, their tribes, their clans, or family relations by whatever name the same way. Thus, brothers need to respect the fact that all human beings who bleed the same way, have human rights that are inherent, which cannot be legislated or taken away from anyone because they are, in the words of a friend of Thomas Jefferson, "God-given." And on teaching her boys these things, she may inculcate certain principles of living that may demonstrate the frustration of families still living in mud after 70 years, while they watch other families sleeping in the homes their fathers built.

History records for all to read that the British started it, because for hundreds of years before that Muslims allowed Jews to live safely from Christian persecution; and the Jews who emigrated to Palestine before Zionism carried knowledge from abroad hoping to make life better for both descendants of Abraham. So why are they fighting? We will know the answer to that question when the Spirit of Peace and Brotherly Love gives it to those who search for the truth.

Broken Promises and Bad Policies

From the historical record of the McMahon – Husain Letters of 1915, there is no-one in Britain or America who can deny or even attempt to refute the fact that the British Government promised the Arabs of the Fertile Crescent Independent Arab Democracies.

Also in this monograph, I have shown that Great Britain was on the hunt to control as much of the world's oil that it could find from the time they transformed the British Navy from steam to oil in 1912. This was evident by the report of Sir Edmund Slade Rear Admiral of the British Navy, who suggested that Britain send out explorers to scour the world for oil, make contracts when they find it, and use that oil for commercial purposes and the plying of worldwide trade, while saving the oil of its colonies for a time of war. Thus, when oil was discovered in Mosul the same year, Great Britain sought to control that oil while it also dominated control of the oil in Southwestern Iran. Consequently, it was an academic exercise that British politicians would seek to control all the oil from Iran to Egypt, especially since the world was at war in 1915.

Early in March 1914 before the war started, British and French representatives at conference in London were making agreements to cooperate with each other in the distribution of Arab Oil by the Turkish Petroleum Company (TPC). Ironically, wither Turkey nor Arabs were represented at the meeting. Now in 1915, with Britain facing a serious military situation for lack of shells – having made a bad military judgment with respect to controlling the battlefield – His Majesty's Government decided to ask the Arabs for help in the war. If the Arabs would join their side against Turkey, Great Britain would guarantee Arab independence on all Arab Lands when the time comes. The only condition was that Britain would be given the economic concessions of the territory. But as the negotiations continued we saw that Britain was hedging for land for France, an issue clearly denied by Sharif Husain of Mecca in his letter.

By late 1916, British politicians became fearful that the Russians might withdraw from the war because the Bolshevik Revolution were threatening to end Tsarist Russia. Thus, Lord Crewe of Britain's Ministry of the Diplomatic Corp, encouraged diplomats in Russia and France to persuade Jews around the world to support Russia's war effort in Exchange for Britain's support for a Jewish homeland. British diplomat Arthur Balfour wrote a letter to Lord Rothschild stating that the British Government would support Palestine as a homeland for Jews if Jews in America could coerce the United

States into the war. It worked, and the US entered the war on the side of Britain and France, especially since she was supplying Britain with supplies and food for quite some time to that point.

Then came 1917 when the Bolshevik Revolution toppled the Tsar and exposed the 1916 Sykes-Picot Secret Agreement in which Britain and France had agreed to divide the German holdings, as well as the territory of the old Ottoman Empire between them. The United States was embarrassed; but the Turks celebrated at the disdain and humiliation the West had dropped on the Arab tribes who had rallied to the British side because of their written guarantees. The British would never again be able to gain the full trust of the isolated Arabs; yet the real sting of the betrayal would not be felt until 1936 and again in 1948.

Winston Churchill's bold denial in 1922 also gave rise to Arab uprisings after Zionists started organizing illegal immigration into Palestine. In addition, those Zionists, whom Britain did allow to migrate into Palestine, began to agitate that Palestinians should be removed from Palestine and resettled in Syria and Lebanon. More than anything, this angered all Muslims everywhere. How could Jews who were allowed to settle in Palestine from Russian slaughter have the audacity to demand that Palestinians should be banned from their place of residence? And to add insult to injury, when Hitler came to power in 1933, hundreds of thousands of Jews fled to Palestine and any place to which they could escape. Consequently, they packed into Palestine and added to the ire of the Palestinians, who were still no closer to the national independence promised them by Great Britain; and because British officials continued to support a Jewish homeland at every turn, the Palestinian Arabs awoke to the reality of Western hatred and lack of concern for their humiliation.

The student asked, "Why are they fighting, and why do they hate us?" In 2004 the *Harvard International Review* published an article entitled *Lifting the Veil: Understanding the Roots of Islamic Militancy* in which Dr. Munson reported the results of a Zogby International survey of 2,620 Muslims in Egypt, Jordan, Lebanon, Morocco, and Saudi Arabia. The results showed that in the opinion of these people, the hostility of Muslim extremists towards the United States had less to do with cultural and religious differences than with US policies in the Arab World and the Middle East.

U.S. President George Bush said in 2001 that the Islamic terrorists hate us because they are religious fanatics and "hate our freedoms." This is untrue. Current US President Donald Trump also echoed this idea on the campaign trail in 2016. But while these leaders have commanded their sycophants to carry this as a talking point, more than a billion Muslims from around the world would disagree. Munson opined that if bad US policies have caused this hostility then it would make sense to change those policies. If, however, the terrorism is the result of religious fanaticism then to use brute force to try to defeat it is completely idiotic and nonsensical. Why would that be? It would be nonsensical simply because such a fanatic wants to die as a martyr.

On the campaign trail, President Trump also said that it may still be possible that Saudi Arabia was involved in the bombing of the World Trade Center. Now, amid a brewing scandal in his own administration, the US President heads for Saudi Arabia, and some pundits are eagerly waiting to see how his visit turns out. They are waiting to see how the visit with the Saudis turn out and what will be accomplished, simply because the world knows that the Taliban Government of 2001 Afghanistan were students of Saudi Arabia's Wahhabism, and the 19 Islamic terrorists that attacked America were members of Osama bin Laden's al Qaeda force who as Wahhabi graduates once petitioned the Saudi Government to allow them to defend Saudi Arabia against the US soldiers stationed there by former President Bush in 1990.

Munson wrote at length to explain that the issue which arouses the greatest hostility among even moderately devout religious Muslims who tolerate the secularism and immodesty of westerners is the Israeli-Palestinian conflict. Eighty percent of those interviewed in 2001 by Zogby International in Egypt, Kuwait, Lebanon and Saudi Arabia categorically blamed the United States for the suffering of the Palestinian people. Later that year in December 2001, the Pew Research Center released a survey, which found that US Policy on the Israeli-Palestinian conflict was the main source of hostility toward the United States. So why are they fighting, and why do they hate us? Could it be that they fight, not to go to Heaven for 72 virgins, but because they have been humiliated and suffer insults, disdain and pain resulting from broken promises, and are held under the steel boots of Israeli brown shirts, and are banned from getting arms with which to fight other than the stones a boy's hand can hurl.

On June 3, 2003, the Pew Research Center released a report entitled *Views of a Changing World.* This study was conducted in April – May 2003 shortly after the fall of Iraq and Saddam Hussein. The survey of sixteen thousand Muslims in 21 countries showed a marked increase in hostility against the United States for the war against Iraq over the survey in 2002 of 38,000 Muslims in 44 countries who were more supportive of the United

States in its retaliation for the 9/11 bombing of the World Trade center. It appears that the farther we get from 9/11, the continued rhetoric of the war-hawks in Congress – on the Republican Right – and the hate crimes against Muslims in America continues to drive upwards the resentment of American-Muslims.

How President Trump expects to wage an all-out war against "Radical Islamic terrorists" when he does not trust his spy agencies who accuses of "fake" news, and wants to ban all Muslims, no doubt including those who speak Arabic and the dozens of dialects of various militant Muslim countries. Perhaps Americans might consider giving open thanks to the thousands of Muslims who risk their lives in the US military and its various spy agencies to ferret out the imminent threats against America and American citizens. When the Religious Right who claim to have family values, come to understand that Jews in a certain city were more Christian than the Christians when they rushed to scrub hate-filled graffiti from the mosque, maybe they would come to understand the tenets of their Faith.

In similar fashion, I stood the next week and saw Muslims who rushed to the aid of the Jews to wash the walls of the synagogue. Is this not what Jesus meant when He said that men should love one another? Perhaps, a new generation of students would get to know the truth, and refuse to listen to the lies of greedy politicians who refuse to acknowledge even one act of good, believing that to do so would cost them a vote or two. Such a man or woman is not deserving of one vote, and certainly not the respect reserved for leaders of the Free World.

ABOUT THE AUTHOR

Dr. Kenneth Adderley was born the eldest son of a Baptist minister in Nassau, Bahamas. At the age of sixteen he matriculated to college in the United States and four years later was engaged to serve at the United Nations as a junior diplomat (International Relations) for the Uganda Mission to the United Nations.
Seven years later after resigning his government posts, Adderley returned to graduate school and earned a Master of Divinity from Andrews Theological Seminary, followed by a Master of History from the University of Memphis, and a Doctorate from Capella University. He taught on the University level for more than 20 years before retiring.

Recently, he has served as Chairman of the Mid-West Educational Research Association Department of History & Historiography (MWERA), Affirmative Action Chair of the Black Hawk Democrats, and as an Adjunct instructor for Hawkeye Community College. He Serves now as Director of Christian Education for the Iowa Missionary & Educational Baptist State Convention, and has authored several monographs to help young people in their search for truth.

Learning the ins and outs of British diplomacy and politics (Bahamian Independence Talks London 1972).

www.ingramcontent.com/pod-product-compliance
Ingram Content Group UK Ltd.
Pitfield, Milton Keynes, MK11 3LW, UK
UKHW020135250726
13967UKWH00002B/677

9 781548 960384